SHE OF THORN

I0158046

Poems and Prose by

KALYNN CAMPBELL

TORN APART BOOKS

Orders by U.S. trade bookstores and wholesalers. Please contact:
Torn Apart Books
Los Angeles, Caifornia
www.tornapartbooks.com

All Rights Reserved
Printed in the United States of America

First Printing: March 2015

ISBN-13 978-0692407431

Category: Poetry, Prose

1-10987654321

subtle
does not
a hammered heart
break

INTRODUCTION

*W*hat you hold in your hands is a love story.

Look closely. Through the vexed tossing of wrathful words and acerbic rhymes, a bittersweet truth emerges. Yes, what follows is nothing more than a woeful love story wistfully told by a broken, battered, and oft angry heart.

This book constitutes the last chapter of a volatile and at times destructive relationship. It did not start that way but neither was the beginning a simplistic love affair. No, it was not of pastel paper hearts and picturesque marigolds neatly folded in the bright envelope of spring. It was of shared damage and a soul mate deep connection tightly wrapped in a stained brown bag of off balance love. For it was an affair in the purest sense of the word. A taboo matrimonial whisper. As such, I learned to live among shadows.

I had not known such deep and profound love for a woman before the she of these poems. Together we created a world rivaled only by the Elysian Fields. After just over a year of fervent passion, things changed. Mournfully, her love for me died, but she did not let loose of love's umbilical cord. Why I was kept tethered to a one-sided connection, a connection that fused my beating heart to her dead one, I will never know. I only know she grew cruel during this period. The truculence twisted my soul, killing me slowly day by brutal day. My only outlet was the *SHE OF THORN* poems.

What an abysmal thing love can be.

A sad truth is contained in the words, 'When all is said and done there was always more that could have been said and done.'
With *SHE OF THORN*, perhaps enough has been said.
And done.

Kalynn Campbell

SCENT

She of past
in silence creeps
her scent
lightly
breathes
on me

soft is breath
of broken
promise
strong the
scent
of
forget-me-nots

drifting
faintly
through me
a redolence sedates
then asphyxiates
from pink
of envelope
seduced
in purple ink
She creeps
silently seeps

deliberately
her scent

breathes
on me

THE MOON
BECOMES A SLIVER

my shadow fell
kissing the ground
it shimmered like glitter
to touch the low
I am not alone
even the moon
becomes a sliver

how long did I drown
words choking
as rapids in a river
to quietly die
I am not the first
even the moon
fades to a sliver

my shadow cries
broken by light
"hallelujah!"
yells a sinner
one man's light
is another's dark
when the moon
becomes a sliver

I POUR YOUR NAME

every night
I pour your name
as if these eyes
do not see
I reach
for the what is not
and never will be
and deliberately

pour them
over me

now ritual
to spill your name
toast your discarnate
a love in vain
this sickness
my head-hanging shame
as another glass
of your name
I deliberately pour

over me

of you I reek
although I can't abstain
as the damp corrodes
so grows the stain

to die alone
the price I pay
to knowingly

pour you

over me

DEAD MAN WALKING

I am
the dead man
walking
through you

I am
that 'what if'
of the mind
the hidden picture
he soon finds
an unspoken name
a muted white lie
mine is the face
never in place

the dead man
in your heart

I am
that man

the dead man
walking
through you

LAYER BY LAYER

one layer past
where I once fell
one layer past
I found myself
one layer past
I once cared
one layer past
the layer we shared

harder the skin
each layer grows
and layer by layer
the magic slows
yet layer by layer
I layer my Shell

until layer by layer
I've deadened
myself

MY WOUNDS

I salt my wounds
for if they heal
I will forget

and She will
return

to open new ones

THE STAIN

I remember a time
you smiled
when I was around
the stain
only a spill
you were fragile then
and I was strong
before the stain
set in

we always caught us
before we dropped
long before
the stain
was even
a spot

before the fights
before the pain
soiled our beings
marking us
forever
stained

I think of our
spills
and how they
seeped
covering us
until the stain
left us both
weak

but what could we do
destined
even preordained
once we were spilled
we would always
carry the
stain

THE FORGOTTEN

I am the familiar
of me you once knew
you try hard to place me
something hard to do
I am the once but gone
of the forsaken I drip
I am the not remembered
a shadow in an eclipse
I will always haunt you
the misplaced name and face
for I am the forgotten
a soul you once erased

I BURIED HER

I buried her in the field today
there was no sun
there was no rain
the sky as She, dark gray

I buried her in the field today
She is not near flowers
She is not near weeds
her grave is lost
like She left me

I buried her in the field today
I spoke no words
I had nothing to say
I simply did as She
I walked away

WE'VE GONE TO SLEEP

we've nothing to say
there's nothing to share
we've both gone to sleep
we no longer care

look at us now
nothing is left
love for each other
we do not possess

there is no grave
nor urn to keep
not even a eulogy
for our endless sleep
nothing can wake us
we can't even dream
it's time to leave us
resting in peace

and should I wake
once we're apart
may I never find sleep
in another's heart

SHE WAS TORN

She was torn
folded tight
a letter of longing
longing reply

heart of paper
love forlorn
on my table
She
laid torn

so easy She frays
quietly tears
silently crumbles
a heart
of despair

gently I hold
glueing up tatters
stitching with
needles
mending with
patches

on my table
from folds
her heart
lovingly laced
alive
in my hold

She
letter of longing
for me

unfolds

MY TATTOO

I made her my tattoo
in my skin She remains
with death She is company
but in life She is in vain

our corpse I embrace
a pious love once was
a memory thick with rot
and acerbic dust

I worship a ghost
I pray a hollow god
I am as I believe
so towards the grave I plod

She will not save me
She buried me long ago
but where is the truth
in reaping what we sow?

tattooed on my skin
like a window to hell
is my act of repentance
and the reason I fell

HER MEAN SEASON

eye for an eye
tear for a tear
reason for reason
no reason to care
quickly time passes
as quick as the tears
it falls like a hammer
her mean season is
here

bitter the voice
nasty the fight
long is the day
longer the night
easy to tell
by the hastened chill
there's blood on the
moon
her mean season is
here

HER BLOOM

She, a rare bloom.
angelic, alluring.

curious, was I.
forbidden, was She.
rebel, I am.

I picked her.

SHE IS AS WATER

She is the pool
my body is found
She is the lake
I so often drown
hers is the ocean
my body drifts
swallowed whole
with a salty kiss

to fight her current
I need not bother
for She is as water
She pulls
me
under

her smile a vertex
eyes an undertow
She is my siren
an anchor of woe
why does her hold
steal my breath?
why must it always
end in my death?

I know the answer
I need not wonder
for She is as water
She pulls
me
under

SHE IS MY SHAME

I now ever sullen
on her I place blame
She is of regret
the birthmark of shame

yes, it was I
who gave of my soul
for such a reckless act
I pay a heavy toll

to her
deceit but a game
stealing of my dignity
leaving only shame

love long faded
yet I touch of flame
every word here burns
the brimstone of shame

should this She find you
hold steady to your way
or live forever low
the penance, the shame

WHERE IS THE SHE

where is the She
who did this to me

cut to the quick
twisted the knife
then without word
disappeared
in the night

She of thorn
herself absorbed
behind She leaves
nothing of worth

look at me now
my life is as his
for without her
my heart is dead

back to him
She took it all
leaving me here
to beg and crawl

so tell me this
then I'll let it be
where is the She
who did this to me

PATRON SAINT OF SUNSETS

another death
She gifts
today
of sunsets
She is Patron Saint

wings of sorrow
halo of goodbye
not meant
for tomorrow
so today
it will die

grieving her
beauty
I expire on her
lips
hard goes
the fall
of an
unanswered
wish

from the sky
She drops
my soul
into dirt
an end to pain
but never
the hurt

She is death

dropping
without restraint

of sunsets
She is Patron Saint

THINGS OF MY SOUL

with needle of dark
the night my tattoo
under pale skin
bleeds a sonnet of blue

I look up to heaven
It's no longer there
in the world of night
I've learned not to care

stars shine dark purple
each deep as a bruise
constellations of bone
touch the corpse of a moon

an ambulance waits
what it takes it will keep
these the things of my soul
when my heart falls asleep

THE ALREADY GONE

of mine She is not
our future not long
in briefness I kiss
the already gone

her arms a reminder
i've known all along
it's memory I hold
in the already gone

of life all around
I do not belong
so it is I embrace
the already gone

I ask no forgiveness
I pay for the wrongs
every time I lose
the already gone

THE RIDE

She saw he did not belong
so She offered him a ride.

he saw She belonged
so he let her drive on.

HER CLOUD

her cloud
was not black with pain
it did not cry out
with cold woeful rain
her cloud
was not white with joy
it did not excite
like a child's new toy

her cloud
was but simple gray
heavy as carpet
left in the rain
it rolled over her
with a gentle sad
it brought her down easy
into a nightshade bed
each day She wore it
wrapped as a cape
it brought out her eyes
and the pale of her face

it was her love
I could not compete
for I was a shadow
I stopped at her feet
to cast a presence
was never allowed
to do so would mean
the death of her cloud

so it shall be
just her and the gray
the two now forever
master and slave

I AM HIM

I am the ghost
She locks in her house
once I was me
who became him somehow

She calls me his name
"remember?" She'd ask
while showing me pictures
from some birthday past

before I knew it
I had filled his shoes
I matched him perfectly
down to the tattoos

now the person I was
has already dimmed
I am no longer sure
i'm not really him

so next time we meet
call me his name
because he and I
have become
one in the same

HER DREAMS

She grew her dreams
without roots.

they fell hard

in the first
soft
wind.

HER FACE

i've not seen her face
for over forty days
it is only in memory
upon it I gaze

as beautiful as a flower
yet as sad as a death
it had known hardships
and stolen breaths

it lived a few lifetimes
even gathered some scars
it built wells of wishes
leveled acres of hearts

it had a few secrets
and many dark lies
yet it shone like a ruby
a nirvana with eyes

no, I have not seen it
for over forty days
and that is a gift
for I once was it's slave

SHE IS AN EXECUTION

I am given no menu
wants, She does not care
She is an execution
and this my last meal

She serves up bitterness
on a plate of my detest
a side of wretchedness
and a bowl of discontent
the feast so foul
poached in ill intent
a serving of abhorrence
a side of pestilence
a chilled glass of despise
I drink down with zeal
it no longer rips me
i'm too numb to feel
as I fight the fetidness
I soon get my fill
for She is an execution
and this is my last meal

spoiled from the beginning
it's rotten to the end
I gag on hopelessness
and choke on malcontent
lies garnish the deception
it's quite a sadistic fare
with the smell of putridness
there's grieving in the air
an inevitable death sentence
hope without a prayer
for She is an execution
and this is my last meal

SHE DRAWS
ME IN

although my heart
will not tame
it matters not
She draws me in

a craft honed
her only gift
without words
She draws me in

I, cyclorrhapha
her web disguised
araneae of mine
draws me in

never again
forever I say
never comes never
as my She
draws me in

A SIFT OF
HER

She
a sift
of flower

caressed
kneaded
rose
in
bloom

DOWN SHE
RAINS

clouds cover me
they just won't break

over my shoulder
down She rains

a poisoned name
quietly slips
clouds keep pushing
my soul to eclipse

her storm rolls in
it just won't break

over my shoulder
down She rains

I live as immortal
till the day I die
and sadness I seek
but never know why

clouds cover me
they just won't break

while from my eyes
down She rains

from these eyes

She rains

SHE IS AS HIM

She is not as I
She is as him
cruel
vain
laodicean

She did not come
with such sin
gifts so foul
are bestowed
not birthed

from him
She gladly took
until they covered her
with tar and grime

sealing her in
death

but in me
She sees
herself

before the gifts
before the contempt

before
him

QUEEN OF HEARTS

She built us a house of
cards
then declared herself queen

She built us a castle of
sand
then declared me king

She built us a world of
dreams
then declared it ours

She then fell asleep
and our world

was
gone

HER HOUSE

unbroken windows
fresh is the paint
but doors bolted shut
behind a fetching white gate
it is of her heart
that house down the block
long it stands empty
yet I continue

to knock

BROKE ME

I walked five years
sick on my knees

I watched a soldier
openly weep

I felt loneliness
in a bright holiday

I know what is meant
by *hell to pay*

I've listened
to battered children cry

I held hands
with a soul about to die

I felt them all

deep

to my core

but none
broke me

like her.

tell her She is wrong
this is not her love song

19

BUT A LEAF

with a

chill

in the wind

slowly

She turns
again

in a graying
sky

a calico

goodbye

the last
to drop

in this

the season

of our

fall

I SPIT MY HEART

I spit my heart
against the wind
it didn't blow back
I lost it again
off it flew
to a snatching wind
how long before
I see it again?

somewhere it calls
somewhere it's alone
i'm not even sure
it knows the way
home

and if you see it
please be kind
for it's very naive
and somewhat blind

that will teach me
my lesson learned

spit out a heart
end up forlorn

yes I spit my heart
against the wind
it didn't blow back
i'm without again

SHE PULLS ME

in the night
a bright beam
She is a star
She
pulls me

where I stand
and where I go
She is gravity
She
pulls me

in her hands
tied to strings
I am her puppet
She
pulls me

caught on a line
in a dead sea
on her hook
She
pulls me

I am an annual
gone to seed
up by the roots
She
pulls me

HER LOVE, A DEATH

her
love,
a death

once
vital

of living
shell

quickened

impassioned

a
love
shed

departed

lies

empty
lifeless

a keepsake
memento
shelved

forever
rests
the death

that is

her
love

THE LEAVING KIND

She was the leaving kind
suitcase at the ready
coat within reach

She left me often

of days She was gone
I counted

with every leaving
her return stay
became that much
longer

it was clear

if She left
one more time

She would be

mine

THE ONLY TIME

the only time She loved me
was when She hated her.
the only time She looked for me
was when She lost her.
the only time I was lonely
was when I was alone
with her.

SHE OF HERSELF

She is not of earth
She is not of sea
She is of herself
and will always be

and to herself
She is the chosen one
there is none better
perfection is done

She created her beauty
sculpted her dream
and in her image
demands we believe

She gives to no one
for everyone takes
yes, She is a goddess
all others are fake

for having greatness
She is quite naive
we must not question
only believe

to tell her the truth
is cruelly unkind
for She is an island
self exiled in mind

She is not of fire
She is not of sky
She is of herself
and to herself
She lies

SHE OF SILK

She of silk
wrapped in lace
draped in moon
held in chaste

a child of touch
a mother of feel
twice of heaven
this She of silk

now to herself
her world alone
falls her dreams
in drops of hope

a forgotten one
lives here still
no, he can't see
his She of silk

laced in sorrow
of her I write
for sad is silk

when long
is
night

HER DRUG

sadness, her drug
it only took
a tear

SHE WATCHES ME

forgive me love
for I have sinned
I led her here
once again

stalking my steps
her scent in the wind
with odious eyes
hair of red
She of thorn
watches me

a fixed look
drips with touch
licks my nape
sniffs my wound
studies pain

icepick deep
eyes creep
She of torment
She of thorn
watches me

her stare
an affixation
my choking
a hanging
my strangling

She of thorn
hair of red
eyes of green
beyond those trees
watches me

it isn't enough
to own my heart
to see me crawl
watch me fall
witness me bleed

on me
her eyes of greed
feeds
for I am prey

with look of knives
She waits
with want
to slaughter me

somewhere
there
beyond the trees

She
watches me

THE SCREAM

as if a voice
a loud scream
I hear her face
in every dream

I cover my ears
but still it looms
I can not quiet
the face in the room

her dead eyes
not as they seem
they choke my soul
with every scream

comes a day
tables turn
when I loom
as the face in her
room

HER
GRAVITY

her
gravity was
stronger

than my
will

to fly.

PRISONER OF SELF

She spoke of him
how her heart he held
it haunted her still
sad prisoner of self

the sun was gone
burned to the ground
her sky fell empty
not a ray to be found

only in rain
does her world shine
each drop a smile
damp of suicide

She said She lamented
the passing of time
with all that was taken
and that left behind

I touched her chest
her heart beat slow
he stabbed too hard
She was letting it go

I was no comfort
although I tried
it did no good
her heart soon died...

She spoke of him
how her heart he held
it haunted her still
sad prisoner of self

SWEET NOTHINGS

sweet are the nothings
no longer here
for nothing is lost
when nothing is near
bitter are nothings
with nothing to give
and sad are nothings
we constantly send
then there are nothings
that long make a night
if nothing is wrong
then nothing is right
but are not all nothings
like the nothing of smoke?
to see there is nothing
gives something
some
hope

SHE IS

She is simple
because it is not hard

She is weak
because it keeps her strong

She is sad
because it makes her happy

She is here
because it is not there

She is her confused one...
She is my predictable one.

HER MIRROR

She looks in the mirror
and leaves life behind
She loses herself
as if She's enshrined
for hours She stands
like She can not see
her head does not move
not a single degree

yes deep in the mirror
She buries her eyes
not once do they blink
as if She has died
life can be be ugly
beauty disguised
but there in her mirror
a second life lies...

one day She'll fall
into silver glass
from this world to that
She will quickly pass
into the reflection
her soul will go
and her mortal world
will matter no more

so if at her mirror
I call out for She
will She look back
or will it only be me?
And if I keep staring
will I feel some bliss
or will the reflection
be only our sadness

I TOUCHED BLUE

She spoke of 'sorry'
yet little I care
the color of remorse
not as it appears

in gray I fell
in white I flew
my fingers bled black
when I touched blue

swallow of ocean
clouds having died
all this in a color
the color of goodbye

no longer red
tendresse subdued
my heart fell black
when I touched
blue

HER LOVE

her love -
like witnessing
a slow
sinking
ship

fascinating
yet
terrifying

as
it slips
away

SHE WHO BROUGHT SADNESS

only She who brought sadness
can take it away

but She has gone missing
and left me in chains
a prisoner of self
in a downpour of rain
tattoo of despair
a handshake with pain
I wander the night
to find her I pray

only She who brought sadness
can take it away

there are two levels
upon which we stroll
one is the intellect
the other the soul
but just in between
a place called 'desire'
an inferno of fire
like a funeral pyre

it is here I am
stuck between floors
wishing to leave
yet crying for more
eternity in sorrow
I am doomed to pay

only She who brought sadness
can take it away

LIFE OUT LOUD

not lost but never found
peering in but never out
they forget you're there
living quietly out loud

never doing what is vowed
always stuck in self-doubt
you missed it all
living quietly out loud

when you wish upon a fear
the wishing gods don't hear
and hollow is a life
lived quietly out loud

life is short is wrong
life this way is long
only the very strong
live quietly out loud

lonely you may be
away from all the crowds
but you are not alone
living quietly out loud

(for the Avpd)

FLEETING

the ephemeral was today
while gone the never stays
for but a moment
I touched the for awhile
just before

She went
away

CUTTING MYSELF DOWN

i'm cutting myself down
and leaving behind
the noose She devised
to hold me in binds

no more will I swing
no more will I greave
her tree soon bare
of the soul of me

the roots below
do not reach deep
her love an illusion
I now clearly see
so too this noose
She hangs me with
a heartless power
in a life of anguish

the tree is sickness
the leaves are lies
the sooner I flee
the sooner it dies

i'm cutting myself down
and leaving behind
the tree of suffering
and the She of unkind

SHE KISSES ME

my once She
my used-to-be
my death decree
agony of thorn
torturous queen
She softly
kisses me...

her lips
a quiet plea
stabs
at the scar
as if not there
She softly
kisses me...

I feel her blade
slide deep
but no longer bleed
it's all the same
only numb remains
as She softly
kisses me...

She can not find
her kingdom
her castle of grief
a knife in my heart
lost in the search
She softly
kisses me...

nothing remains
She does not believe
hand in my chest
continues to seek
while on my lips
She softly
kisses me...

there is no lock
or kingdom
of this is key
no longer anchored
I take to sea
with one last drowning
I let her
softly
kiss me...

IN A SATURINE SKY

She speaks in a whisper
a haunting lullaby
as stars begin to fade
in a saturnine sky

the cross we bear
our legacy to the grave
a doleful imprisonment
of the self-enslaved

there are sorrows in night
the day can't conceive
there are foolish dreams
we all want to believe

with belief we can survive
with belief we carry on
in truth we live the pain
until this life is gone

She leaves in a whisper
a tearful lullaby
as stars quietly pass
high in a saturnine sky

HER DAMAGE DONE

I am
beautiful damage

her damage
done

She will
return
for She is
incendiary

feverishly drawn

to the
damage

the
beautiful damage
done

in me

forever
I am
fettered

to the deed

She will
return

a seditious need

for I am the
beautiful damage

the damage
done

is me

SHE SHADOWS ME

through miles of years
i've learned to see
and I see
close behind
my forgotten
shadows me

from the distance
where She lays
quietly
without a peep
She shadows me

a hint of blue
in the color red
a wisp of death
in a nuptial bed
of goodbyes
never said

so it is
gingerly
She shadows me

without a step
She creeps
specter white
watching me

I turn and see
a breath of blue
the forgotten She

quietly
shadows me

SHE SPILLED
AWAY

like summer rain
down She seeps
in tears
She builds
our effigy
soon swept away

a river She
without warning

spills
away
from me

She of his
me of mine
I can not move
unspoken lines
but in heart
I held awhile
She of rain
and broken smile

the time of us
but memory
a time before
She
spilled

away
from me

SHE HAD

She had a scent

it drove me mad
She had a past

it was quite sad
She had a marriage

it made her blue
She had a secret

it wasn't true
She had a temper

it had a bite
She had a truth

it was really a lie
She had a heart

I got to hold
it had no love

so I let it go

I WOULD

I would drive from here
if I could find a road
I would walk from here
if I could find a path
I would cry a river
and paddle from here
if I could find
a tear

KING OF THE BROKEN

I, king of the broken
lord of the lost
the down-turned trodden
the souls of mistrust

on land now burned
a kingdom in ruin
the damage done
there is no undoing

we live in bleakness
nothing rebuilt
a reason for caring
long ago killed

this is the land
of pain and grief
a kingdom comprised
of funeral wreaths

and I am but king
lord of the broken
the ruler of woes
forever unspoken

HER RANDOM ACT

She says She loves you
words deeply sublime
you don't even notice
the random act
of unkind

her lies you believe
you ignore all signs
you are soon to become
her random act
of unkind

your back She stabs
it shows in her eyes
you've just become
her random act
of unkind

I EVAPORATE

to die in darkness
this I contemplate
for without the sunrise
I will evaporate

of love She steals
nothing left to take
if She leaves me now
I will evaporate

should he take her back
as though it is of fate
like hope to the broken
I will evaporate...

the sunrise is missing
for me it is too late
like silk of morning dew
slowly I evaporate

KALYNN CAMPBELL

I AM FOR KILLING

She of borderline smile
and narcissistic heart
licks at stumbled vows
addled with abandonment
hungers for the taste
of remembrance
and I
lonely fool of swine
lies at her plate
the sacrificial pig
my loins primed
She cuts at missing ribs
duplicity never tender
it's bouquet meaty of
waiting rooms and
take-a-number butcher shops
I, starter of pally
a side of advantage
She takes of me
salting with a burn
my sweet devoutness
food for vanity
my lonely soul, nosh
fork deep in chest
knife firm in back
ladled with thick nothings
soon a forgotten bite
I am leftovers
surplus staples
a plate of wonted
like time
I am for killing
while She waits
at a table
for
him

SHE WAS A LOSS

She was a loss
right from the start
a penny soon dropped
love without heart

I would not listen
I stared at the sun
I ran with scissors
I wallowed in fun

like all cheap things
we were made to break
our love soon spoiled
like mold on a cake

but yes I would
I would do it again
what is a thrill
without a little sin

and truth be told
when life wears thin
sometimes the heart
needs an easy win

MY TODAYS

my todays think
they are yesterdays
they can not conceive
of tomorrow
so it is I look behind
to see a future

THERE IS

there is a rain
that does not chill.
there is a tear
that is not sad.
there is a love
that does not hurt.
somewhere
there is.

somewhere.

WITH PAPER AND PEN

in between the lines
a nasty heartless lie
drops me to the ground
the shot without sound
with paper and pen
I touched sadness again

they say the wind cries
for those about to die
then push me in the storm
and bid me a goodbye
for with paper and pen
I touched sadness again

SHE RESURRECTS ME

She of flame
my torch
uncrowned
queen
She lights
my phoenix rising
She
resurrects me
into the ground

blistered
scorched
up I go
no savior
nor angel be
but a demolition
She resurrects me
into the ground

condemned
I must repeat
the burn
third degree
dipped in kerosene
drowned in brine
She resurrects me
into the ground

with silence
She lights
her stare
ignites
in red
She burns
without a sound
my phoenix rising
She
resurrects me
into the ground

THE CONNECTION

The connection you share. It is a deep one.
It is like a jungle vine growing from your chest to theirs.
This is the hold.
This is the reason you know them as deeply as you do. This
is the reason you ache with such voracity. This is the abysm
from which the suffering comes.
You decide it must be pulled free.
You start by yanking it by the roots. This is easier said
than done. The roots are hopelessly wrapped and tangled
around your helpless heart. The more you pull the more the
heart is torn with lacerations and abrasions as the roots try
desperately to keep hold. The harder you tug the tighter it
grabs. It knows this is the life-force and without the heart it
will meet it's demise. Yes it knows this.
You clench both hands around it like a vice grip, your eyes
streaming salty tears as you tug with all your might. It fights
you. This goes on until you think you can take no more when
suddenly, with a last determined pull, it rips free. Memories
pour from the gaping chest wound. They drip and pool at
your feet. The connection is out.
It is over.
You stand stunned. The roots are moving like blades of saw-
grass in a wind storm urgently trying to grab hold of the
heart once more. It screams for you to place it back into your
chest, shrill panicked screams of desperation. The screams are
deafening, sickening, and you feel your stomach twist.
You drop the connection to the ground. It is now frantic like
a fish flopping on a hot pier, gasping for air while the sun
unmercifully beats down on it. It is dying. You can do nothing
but quietly weep.
It is a profound loss. You feel it beyond your heart, deeper
than your core.
You feel it in your soul.
It is empty personified.
Is is your twin.
It is you.
And it is dead.

QUIETLY WE FADE

her presence is weak
a mirage of a blur
once possessor of me
I, possessor of her

lost in my history
removed by assent
quietly we fade
never crossing again

you, now busied
with words of me
all of this here
triviality

there is no always
just perpetual end
as forever we fade
never crossing again

how much beauty
in an ounce of pain
and how much hate
in an ounce of shame

it all falls alike
into a great abyss
when quietly we fade
never crossing again

MY EARTH

I tilled
out the past

sowing it
with new
beginnings.

but soon they
withered
and died.

in a handful
of dirt

I readily
saw why...

She salted
my earth

before
her final

goodbye.

WITH LOVE

with wings
She'll leave

with dreams
She'll fly

with desires
She'll soar

with love

She'll return

AN ODD MOMENT

such an odd moment
when heartache fades
as if one's deceptive
to one's own ways

did She mean nothing?
was I simply a fool?
such are the questions
the heart runs through

but in the dulled end
some lesson was gained
yes, such an odd moment
when heartache fades

40 STORIES

40 stories I stand
40 stories high
40 stories I fall
40 reasons why

40 stories She told
all 40 were lies
each I count
sun in my eyes
reflections on glass
quickly
10 stories pass

30 stories
each I know
each I leave behind
tears as feathers trail
with 30 goodbyes
I spread my arms
and towards them
fly

20 stories
too numb to recite
so I take the twenty
with me in flight
as I put my hand
over my heart
to remember why

10 stories
all ten
start and end
with love enslaved
so for these ten
I now fall
solitary
through space

5 stories
remain
I try to forget
but my
broken life
continues to fly
counting away
all five

1 story
the very same one
without a word
without a sound
She leaves
as I
hit
the ground

TRUTH IS A
PERCEPTION

voices fade to whispers
shadows fade from trace
again my path crosses
desire's abstruse grace

right and wrong is solemn
yet they are the obtuse
a deed has no wrong
when right is of a truth
for long remains memory
after moments slip away
and hungry grows a heart
when it has lost it's way

yes truth is a perception
it is never absolute
biased comprehension
bending belief to truth

and truth now the blinder
as down the track I race
through a turn of desire
into the arcanum of fate

HER WORLD

remind her

if her world were
perfect

She would not
be in it

I AM HER ECHO

I am her echo
haunting
distant
lost

her echo
mine
forever
I die

her voice
tossing me
away
in name

thrown in
darkness
discarded
I fade

no one hears
the wound's
remnant cry

a cry never to
heal
mend
cicatrize

only continue
to bleed
into
the night

her echo
mine

haunting
distant
lost

forever
I die

47

STOLEN MOMENTS

She brought me
stolen moments
a few each day
I spent them
some on me
but most on her
days became months
soon the months years
then one day
She no longer
brought
stolen moments

both
were gone

then he
appeared

he had come for the
moments

moments
we had stolen
from him

THE STAMP

I trekked over fractured addresses
trudged across smeared ink
forged through torn envelopes
prowled deep into faded pastel sheets
even stumbled over thickets of
fragmented regards.
then I found it. the stamp.
but my journey was in vain.
it lay cancelled.

SHE FLEW TO ME

She came one night
a weeping thing
through my window
with broken wings

flew to me

She of wound
came to stay
until the cold
called her away

his grasp
a cage of hold
without wings
never again

will She

fly to me

She of wound
a weeping thing
now of cage
locked in gray

She hides
the reason why
once
with broken wings
She flew

to me

NO PLACE I HAVE
NOT DIED

no, there is no place
I have not already died...

here is where I died from her silence
there is were She killed me with words

over there She used a mocking smile
or was it a sarcastic slur?

about here She used him as a weapon
the same place She failed to care

exactly there She made a promise
but soon broke it over here

and where you are standing
She stabbed a last goodbye

no
there is no place
I have not
already
died

MY APPENDIX

She has become
my appendix.
I only keep her
to avoid
getting
scarred.

INDIFFERENCE

She cut my wrists
with my own
indifference.
that will teach me
to care.

OF YOUR RELIGION

you said of the truth
it was a sole religion
but like a false God
your truth was rewritten

now your religion
is pestilently tainted
your church far from holy
your soul far from sainted
you sing of your praises
versed hymns of unclean
of narcissistic martyrs
baptized in gasoline
you're a failed communion
a wafer of despair
a kiss of vinegar wine
a death-row prayer

no, you are no saint
nor an evangelist star
you are but a stigmata
from heart surgery scars
and I once the believer
so blind I could not see
how hard you would kick me
when I was on bended knees

I now close your testament
I burn all your lies
I bury your religion
in the book of goodbye

SHE OF THORN HANGS

an infant is She
her petty ways
superficially shallow
self-centered always
I saw how She played
with greed for eyes
moves of deceit
shamefully lies

She once set a noose
to watch me hang
but I was not there
as She called my name
I sent He of Thorn
He took my place
He is as She
a wretched case

She loved the bad
drawn to his hell
as weak as I
She of Thorn fell
She gave up her heart
to a thorn of beard
loving a mirror
She let herself care
caught by her game
it's all the same
in a noose set for me
She of Thorn hangs

when blood is sown
blood we must reap
humiliation hers
She kisses his feet
a tune far from sweet
in anguish She sings
'In a noose set for you
I now hang'
without empathy
I watch her swing
melancholy is hers
the queen has a king
my curse is no more
the death bell rang
the cruel She of thorn
in a noose for me
hangs

WHAT SHE IS

what She is
is what She is not
this I see

She is no moon
She shines no beam
softly down on me
She is not gravity
She does not hold
tightly onto me

She
but a star of self
from her heavens
like debris
fell into me
She created
my world
void of beauty

for She gave me
no deep blue sky
only a burning sun
which quickly died
She gave me
no ocean deep
only a barren heart
that does not beat

her truth I now see
She is a universe
without need
of an
insignificant world
like me

WASTED WORDS

wasted words
down by the grave
wait to die
not one i'll save

these words
stain of spurn
taste of hate
although they burn
I hold them in

words I keep
but do not speak
of my soul
they slowly eat

wasted words
i'll never say
wait for me
down by the grave

A LESSON

yes my spoon holds
only pain and ache
the bowl always full
of my many mistakes

say you want to possess
my bone and ash
so toss me to the wind
see if I blow back

nothing is worth much
where nothing will last
just as desires of today
tomorrow all pass

so toss me to the wind
and see if I blow back
should I not return
a hard lesson learned
your spoonful now
earned

PETALS

She pulls
away petals
until She
loves me.

not.

SHE FEELS ALONE

She has a side
She never shows
even with him
She feels alone

something broke
along the way
where went her soul?
She can not say
there must be a hole
or maybe a crack
wherever it went
it will not be back

to be so empty
a despairing plight
a shroud of sorrow
She does not fight

for very deep down
close to the core
is a smile a day
no less and no more
She does not use them
they are blue skies
She saves them up
for a beautiful life

She has a side
She never shows
even with her
She feels alone

THE LAND OF GOODBYE

She thinks I don't know
but I do
She thinks I won't go
but I will
there are no rules
in the land
of goodbye

WRAPPED IN BLUE

the sun rose with yellow
glow
I hid, wrapped in blue

the sun beamed with
orange radiance
I hid, wrapped in blue

the sun dropped in red
tantrum
I hid, wrapped in blue

the night engulfed with
colorless void
I belonged,
wrapped in me

A SONG OF WOE

I sing a song
of pain and grief
a woeful song of
GONE IS She

lonely am I
lonely I'll be
without her
sadness is me

I sing this song
for fallen things
on fallen hearts
the fallen grieve
and down am I
on fallen knees
the ghost of her
strangling me

lonely am I
lonely I'll be
without her
sadness is me

in true rhyme
forever be
this song of woe
will sing in me

HER SECRET

I would never tell
your secret

your terrible lie

the truth you jar
with a walk
that stammers
and crawls

thick
with malcontented lust

and candied breath

as you climb
my body

planting shovels
into a hungered past

hymnals
screaming
from sullen eyes

tombstones
burgeoning
from cold fingers

unholy lips
tonguing my glorious
eulogy

as you lay
dripping

of
his

SHE OF DARK

She of night
of dark
with stars
like skin
a moon of sad
imbedded within
to be as day
bright as sky
not as dark
She
questions why

a wish made
on falling dreams
for falling stars
will fall
too far

when She woke
of earth
was She

planted
firm
life as tree
although of life
not as it seems
for from the seed
goes a weed

branched sad
willowed
with root of weep
her tender shoots
fell incomplete

under rotting bark
a splintered heart
to her knees
like sullen leaves
She slowly
drops

lost of earth
lost of sky
in a sunset
this her time
for always
as She fears

not in earth
not in sky
but of dark
dark of
night

THE MISSING GOODBYE

up on a bridge
you tied a noose
from a rope of spurn
you pushed me loose
never once
did you say goodbye
nothing but silence
as I dropped and died

how many months
have I hung in vain
to hear some remorse
for all this pain
a fool is a fool
and a fool I am
this fool has learned
so never again

here is your rope
save it for him
then think of me
as he swings in the wind

the day will come
a noose around you
and you will at last
hang in my shoes
and I will be there
not to decry
but to give you
this missing

goodbye

A POUND
OF FLESH

a pound of flesh
She cut from me
under the water
so I would bleed

a lake of red
for a body blue
a tub of crimson
for a heart untrue
her words cold
as was the deed
as is the lake
in which I bleed

a pound of flesh
She cut from me
wrapped up tight
in a death decree
my shallow grave
this lake of red
I drink of brine
in every breath

a pound of flesh
She cut from me
deep enough
so I would bleed

SHE SAID
GOODBYE

She said goodbye
as if
pulling a weed

I had become
nothing more
than
an intruder
a nuisance
an unwanted
pest

in a tiny plot
of dirt
She called

her
heart

SHE OF MUERTE

of death She taught me
they are one in the same
She didn't so much
say -
as chisel
my name

SHE OF ABSENCE

She of absence
She of gone

left this soul
here alone

a kiss stolen
as was a heart

now and ever
forever apart

She of absence
never returns

this a lesson
I have learned

She of gone
will not call
mine is not
hers at all

love of black
heart of blue
a rope and prayer
no less will do

in dark
life subdued

I the gone

of absence
too

YOU INTRIGUE ME

a million miles away
in a whisper you say
"I'm alone"
you intrigue me

a drop of obsession
hints of transgression
with so few words
you intrigue me

the distance of sparks
is a touch in the dark
I feel you reach
to intrigue me

written in rhyme
are bookmarks of time
here lies a time
you intrigued me

TO HAVE HER

She is the kind
you will never own.
the kind
who will always
belong to another.
that is the only way
to have her.

KALYNN CAMPBELL

SHE OF THORN

acrid
the life
She feeds me
yet of more
to her
I plead

bitter is thorn
that sweetly drips
the poisoned hold
of an impure fix
her sting of thorn
sharply slips
into me

through the body
head and soul
She spreads
and I
but a fool
begs

stung in thorn
lashed of tongue
I return
again and again
a dependence
to outlive
I have no wish
I can not kick

for somewhere deep
hidden from me
in blue thorns
of morose
blooms
a red
diaphanous
rose

SUCH A PLACE

I slept two years
and never saw a dream

I cut out my heart
and it continued to bleed

I lived life in daylight
and never saw the sun

I walked ninety nine miles
but traveled only one

I threw a never ending party
yet ended up alone

if there was such a place
I would make my way
home

if there was such a place

I would already
be home

I WILL

speak
I will hear

wave
I will see

smile
I will feel

cry
I will
break

SHE SCARES ME

She cuts
but does not care
She bleeds
but does not hurt
She drowns
but does not die
She shows a heart
but does not love
She has me
and that

scares me.

BLACK SUNDAY

it was on a black sunday
and of this I confess
I am guilty of longing
She of the rest

for on that black sunday
wrists cut with thorn
I invoked her ghost
then fell in the storm

yes, on that black sunday
She heard cries of woe
She rushed to possess
this lonely once more

I danced with her dead
arms wrapping me tight
only a trail of ashes
any clue She had died

when She kissed me
past deception I felt
the grave can not hide
a truth once withheld

I slit my heart open
tried to bleed her away
She only held closer
She intended to stay

I dropped on my knees
but it was futile to pray
nothing could help me
on the blackest of days

perpetually I grieve
and for my soul I cry
for on that black sunday
I once again died

IT OF RIDDLE

it lies in a riddle
it lives in a dream
it is the sole reason
to be is to be

they say we need it
but many don't see
it has a grim darkness
that drops in degrees...
yesterday warm
tomorrow it chills
today it makes children
that one day will kill

it is called *love*
and with it comes *hate*
there is no indifference
when love is the fate
it demands respect
or quickly it turns
from a thing of beauty
to a long suffering burn

so take of this heed
or love comes today
to dig a hole deep
for tomorrow's grave

SHE SPILLED
AWAY

like summer rain
down She seeps
in tears
She builds
our effigy
soon swept away

a river She
without warning

spills
away
from me

She of his
me of mine
I can not move
unspoken lines
but in heart
I held awhile
She of rain
and broken smile

the time of us
but memory
a time before
She
spilled

away
from me

OF WEEDS

past the flowers
into weeds
neglected
She grows
me

GRATEFUL

you cut me
to my core

and grateful am I
to love no more

not to again
stumble
or fall

gone
the load
a life supply
I have lived
my last goodbye

nothing to do
but worship you
on an alter
of never
or ever again
not to feel
or care
free forever
of pain

my foe now gone
I celebrate

look at my face
grateful am I
to lose
love's insipid
grace
for I care
no more

so this I say
grateful
am I
you cut me

to my
core

67

TOO MANY ROADS

they told me it was simple
when I got there I would know
they said I can not miss it
but I see far too many roads

how many end at beginnings
how many lead to the grave
how many head for freedom
and how many will enslave
which go straight to fears
and which end at the soul
how many flood with tears
I see far too many roads

they said to follow my heart
mine knows not where to go
with a thousand ways to turn
there are just too many roads

how many lead to compromise
how many add to the load
how many end in sacrifice
are any paved with gold?
how many have no end at all
the answer I will never know
I tried so hard to get back home
but there are far too many roads

YOUR STRING

I am a string
on me you pull
just cut me free
or tie me to you

i'm soon to break
thin is my soul
but loyal I've been
I haven't let go

of this I beg
I even plead
tie me now
or let me be

am I of worth
as your string
red with blood
you refuse to see

you pull me close
when you have need
but where are you
when for you I bleed?

I am your string
on me you pull

cut me
free
or tie me
to you

IN PICTURES

in pictures

I hear
murmurs
tainted
whispers

in pictures

her world
beats
delicately
lonely
desperately

in pictures

She speaks
forlorn
prose

in pictures

her heart
a dying
focus
within

in pictures
She
longs to be
captured

permanently
saved

in pictures

MY PUNK OF
A SOUL

take my ticket to heaven
I earned it in vain
my punk of a soul
is missing again

he wanders the night
he's up until dawn
for days he stays out
I don't see him at all

I ask him to obey
I beg him to stay
twenty times I told him
we were leaving today

take my ticket to heaven
I earned it in vain
my punk of a soul
is missing again

I HAVE

I have a secret
it will never be told
I have a need
it will never be met
I have a fear
it will never leave
I have a truth:
these are things
that
have me

SHE OF EMPTY

deep She aches
a missing key
something gone
a hollow need
leaves her
empty...

today of joy
tomorrow woe
days are seasons
always slow
when She turns
empty...

a scalding rage
her saving grace
it crowds the air
it covers grief
it fills the
empty...

death sometimes
She contemplates
for what is life
when lived in wait
when lived
empty...

this her curse
or something worse
a missing piece
a hollow need
forever She
remains
empty.

SHE OF GEM

her legs
rails of smooth
I ride
under sky
of tattered blue
cloud-bleached
jeans slide
past sun licked
curves
and buckled knees

destination of
diamond mine
soft of orchid
oft dreamed
but not yet seen

sleek rails glide
softly merge
a gentle slide
to valley
warm as fever

to the garden
goes a dreamer
her silken bloom
ruby color
unconfined
I waste
no time
I take of petals
looting veins
robbing stems
rich in ore
I burn of fire
She pink with
sapphire

down I go
in deep
desire

of She
mine

IN DARKNESS

quietly I listen
in darkness
She
breathes
for me

KALYNN CAMPBELL

SHE IS A CLOUD

She is
a volatile cloud

erratic
temperamental

yesterday silken
today storm

thundering ire

black enmity
a typhoon

hailing woes
raining fury

until tomorrows
collapse

crashing down

fragmenting

a fragile
hourglass

of love

spilling me
a grain
at a time

further away

from
her

A WINTER KISS

the winter's kiss
hers

frigidly cold

distant

like stars
and dreams

a season away

lost

in frozen drifts

forever
winter

in her

kiss

A POEM OF ONE

I left her with worries
one for each day

I left her with frets
one for each tear

I left her with strife
one for each hurt

I left her with sadness
one I can't lift

I left her with poems
not one about her

She left me a heart

one that now
breaks

DIDN'T YOU NOW?

hey hey friend of mine
you liked what I had
so you gave her a knife
didn't you now

hey hey girl once mine
you liked who I knew
so you told me a lie
didn't you now

hey hey fool in me
you believed in love
never thought you'd grieve
didn't you now

hey hey good lord above
struggle is strength
so you took them away
didn't you now

hey hey funeral man
you buried them deep
still holding hands
didn't you now

SOUL OF TOMORROW

no messiah
nor martyr be
I, soul of tomorrow
out of place
lost
roaming
in today

misplaced
wandering
without way

seeking that
not yet conceived
a solitary shadow
for perpetuity

hearts held
soon of dust
love goes missing
for the lost

to return ahead
I seek a way

I, of tomorrow
a stranger
lost
in today

a life mislaid
I, of tomorrow
fallen behind

this soul of mine
out of place

ever roaming

lost
in today

HER EYES

if the fire that rages
in her eyes
were captured in a star
the sun would be
a mere
firefly

NOTHING
REMAINS

now that She's gone
not much remains
She took it all
except for the rain

I walked by our place
I wanted to see
if there lived a ghost
of our used to be

from inside voices
two lovers in spat
forced to remember
the remembering sad

for the ghost of us
is the story of ends
a tale of murder
a killing of friends

our good overshadowed
such a broken affair
but to right the wrongs
means I no longer
care

I RIDE

you of beauty
with down-turned eyes
the girl who's hope
so slowly dies
I know where
desires lie
come with me
I ride

you of beauty
with need to hide
craving shadow
but living in light
be his day
i'll be your night
come with me
I ride

you of beauty
a heart that cries
although the sorrow
is justified
there is no death
in what never dies
so come with me
I ride

I WALK ALONE

I dwell in a shadow
to me it is home
I am the loner
I walk alone

I am the stranger
in a group of three
I am the rustle
in a leafless tree
I am the forgotten
among the unknown
I am the loner
I walk alone

we come to this world
with only one soul
and that's how we leave
we own no more

so for this one soul
do not cry or weep
like all the forsaken
that's how it must be

yet still I wander
continue to roam
seeking some wholeness
while walking
alone

THE GRAVEYARD IN
HER CHEST

She came to take me
to the graveyard in her chest.

it was her passion to feel
the crush of unrequited love.

her eyes were bright.
her smile soft.
her kiss tender.
her hold assuring.

I fell for her.

without a word

She left me.

She did not come to take me to
the graveyard in her chest.
She came to make a graveyard

of mine.

IN YOU

in your eyes
I see her stare

in your lips
I feel her kiss

in your voice
I hear her song

in your arms
I hold her near

only in your tears

do I
see you

KALYNN CAMPBELL

THINGS NOW SAID

things now said
things now done
here are the stitches
from where it began

a fool in love
walks blindly through life
and blindly I walked
into her knife

this is the spot
She plunged it in
it twice hit bone
so She plunged again
up to the throat
down to the gut
deep through the chest
how I was cut
no, She was not worth
the misery and pain
yet I let her stab
again and again

what is this sickness
we call of 'love'
and why do we crave
what we should distrust
I have no answers
only these scars
i'll learn from the pain
the rest I'll discard

so why in the end
with such things done
on another's knife
will I again succumb?

I DRIFT AWAY

She of torn and lace
the touch of my disgrace
I an island
lost in place
I drift
further
away

tossed away
a sidewalk dime
a reason
I can not find
to pick me up
so further
away
I drift

buried secrets
once of longing
baptized in dirt
no longer wanting
now an island
further
away
from me

I drift

BEAUTY

god help beauty
when vanity gifts it
a mirror

KALYNN CAMPBELL

YOU OF SORROW

to the world you cover
and try to hide
scars you carry
the damage inside
they do not know
they can not see
just how it feels
how it must be

you of sorrow
made of pain
you of lonely
alone once again
you of tears
a world of rain
you of nothing
no, nothing remains
you of quiet
nobody hears
you of broken
too broken to care
you of empty
it echoes inside
you of fear
too fearful to cry

of what you cover
won't hide who you are
the beauty runs deep
despite all the scars

DID IT MATTER?

now it is over
She but a dream
my world crumbled
had anyone seen?

no,
skies did not fall
heavens did not cry
seas did not part
earth did not die

gods did not notice
or even care
only I
and I alone
shed a lone tear

so it is written
how it must be
to matter to no one
no, no one
but me

HER
FRAGMENTS

She sent
fragments of
herself in the
evening wind

I awoke to the
storm

SHE OF ART

She of art
deconstructed
dark
geometric disorder
luminous
in heart
and pain
multilayered
with
refined chaos
and
abstract structure

She of art
sacred eminence
deconstructed
cryptic trope

a canvas of
subtle
nonentity

She of art
deconstructed
a self-contradiction
an ambiguity
a conundrum

like everything
I once
loved

WHO IS THIS MAN

some are born happy
some are born sad
and some are just born
that's all they have
I am not of them
any of these three
I was born a shadow
so it is for me
my words are simple
but thoughts run deep
I long ago learned
to find, just seek
I've a garden of hearts
they belong not to me
and I own a sadness
it was given by 'She'
though pain I've traveled
and hardships I've known
it doesn't take darkness
for lightness to show
I am as a shaman
there are things I see
but the price of this gift
is I open and bleed
some souls are poems
and some are prose
I am a scribble
a hieroglyph I suppose
so in answer to
"who is this man?"
behind my four walls
I quietly
just am

SHE RUNS
ME DOWN

there is a falsehood
it blows in the wind
She of self
runs me down again

although She is flu
the attack is weak
lacking antibody
so indiscreet
her gossiped lips
quick to condemn
She of self
runs me down again

a bumper of dirt
a road of rage
She ignores the signs
slams to engage
with one last hit
one final attempt
She of self
runs me down again

SWEETEST

sweetest the lips
that kiss
goodbye
first

OF THESE
WORDS

what is the purpose
of these words?
tangled in blue
bordering absurd
born in twilight
dark as night
teeming of loss
and heartache they write

between the lines
there runs a thread
it could be missed
if quickly read

of everything now
nothing will last
so capture the moment
to remember the past
strong is sorrow
as love comes and goes
don't evade feelings
of elation and woe
it's better to scream it
than to live unheard

yes, that is the purpose
of all these words

KALYNN CAMPBELL

SHE OF LETTER

She of letter
came for me

softy tucked
enveloped
slid between sheets
pastel cover
warm with mystique

I pull at seams
damp with kiss
and into the pocket
where She is slid
with a gentle hand
I unfold her breath
a body of words
lies undressed
the scent of urge
strong of longing
a floral caress
cries of wanting

I touch with eyes
now fingers read
sentence by sentence
I glide over She
each line drips
my eyes descend
as word by word
I read her again

She of letter
slid between sheets
with delicate words
came for me

A POEM FOR MY POEMS

pretty
lines
for ugly
words
my mirror
never vain

on tall
stanzas
of bitter
pain
off I plunge
and

hang

saw too much
of me
this time
I toppled
with
post traumatic

rhyme

do not
want
of things

that descend
just
out of

line

of hearts
it is how
they

drop

and where
they

lay

for in a
rhyme
of woeful
words

She's a ledge
in which
the heart
will
fall

away

SLIGHTLY IMPERFECT

born unwanted
She stayed to herself
asked of no one
wished for a prince
hid from the sun
She was
slightly imperfect

She was a good teen
listened to mother
never spoke a word
alone in her world
afraid of the others
She was
slightly imperfect

She liked his indifference
undeserving of love
She wanted his touch
and maybe a kiss
until he left
She never asked much
She was
slightly imperfect

She had a child
who stayed to herself
asked of no one
wished for a prince
hid from the sun
her heart broke
when her child became
slightly imperfect

ill health came calling
She welcomed it in
She was lonely and old
needed the warmth
the world gets cold
when one is
slightly imperfect

long forgotten
when She died
few people came
no one cried
She would not have cared
She learned very young
everything dies
slightly imperfect

HER BED OF WEED

I, once broken
a fallen seed
fell into bed
a bed of weeds

tangled in thorn
I failed to bloom
her bed of weeds
became my tomb
punctured with lies
deep the wounds
if love is dirt
the heart is doomed
but came the rains
a flood of worth
till roots of me
grew past her worst

She of Thorn
now quietly spreads
a hollow heart
on bed of weeds
then waits
for the next
fallen seed

SHE IS BAD LUCK

She is my bad luck
this is her way
everything good
She soon takes away
all of my losses
all the bad breaks
She is the reason
my heart now aches
She is my failing
the shout of "almost"
She is the gremlin
of every "so close"
She is my bad luck
of this I am sure
for only bad luck
could have brought her

LONELY NIGHTS

the nights are lonely
the lonely are holy
the holy are broken
the broken are wicked
the wicked are seductive
the seductive are gentle
the gentle are lonely
the lonely stay lonely
as lonely as the
night

SHE IS MY ADDICTION

She is my addiction
a wretched need

I shoot her
into being
and softly
She bleeds
through me

fingers glide
stroking the blind
gone all identity
a bittersweet benediction
this second coming
of mine

to speak of She
a malediction
so I inject her
without word
a solemn
forbidden rite
of which
I become lord

a like soul
of ritual
She too
feeds

for my desire
my need
my perilous addiction
my She

is now
addicted

to me

A POETIC SNUB

they say I don't fit
the words aren't right
too much like song
too much I rhyme
these snobs of word
they pretend to know
as if they are gods
but their egos show
they poison a truth
they are locked in time
meaningless dribble
they tout as sublime
this is not of all
only a few
but the sad part is
they've gotten to you

I hear your soul
it no longer sings
too busy scribbling
dull pompous things

go with them
with the dinosaurs
close your small world
behind egomaniacal doors
wear your beret
smoke to the stub
choke out the world
with a poetic snub
see where it gets you
yes, let's see how far
what good are the words
if they no longer scar
it is sad to see
this is how you are
I read it in your words
this is how you now
are

I WAIT

They say what drives one away
brings one back someday
I sit

waiting on myself

KALYNN CAMPBELL

SHE IS A SHIMMER

She is a shimmer
a quick glance
a fleeting shadow
light
caught in trance

to have her
would be a slight
a death
to the shimmer
the She of light
to capture her
for and of mine
means the shimmer
will certainly die

I am no hoarder
this heart
will not be undone
by love under glass
pins stabbing
thorax
wings pinned
to wax

so I dance
with the shimmer
make love
to the glance
then ever so softly
let go

of the
trance

SHE BURIED ME

She imprisoned me
a promise at a time

She gave me hope
a lie at a time

She executed me
a kiss at a time

but She buried me
with one simple

goodbye

WOUNDED

She of wound
fragile her need
now safely tucked
wrapped in gauze
of insecurity

why She lives
in her own break
perhaps the care
simply died away

She of wound
fragile her need
the price of want
the reason She bleeds

SHE RUINS EVERYTHING

She ends at the bottom
as it should be
for with malicious intent
She ruins everything

She has no real conscious
her 'wants' trump her
'needs'
like a death at a party
She ruins everything

She lives by deception
hands never clean
like sugar in a gas tank
She ruins everything

She's a true rotten apple
a yard full of weeds
like a slug in the garden
She ruins everything

so why do I love her
when She brings grief
perhaps what I love is
She ruins everything

KALYNN CAMPBELL

THE STORY OF A HEART

She had a red heart
but it turned blue
so She painted it green
that's all She could do
to see a blue heart
filled her with grief
but to own a green heart
brought some relief
there was a reason
her heart turned blue
a black heart broke it
that much She knew
She swore never again
would She feel such pain
so She covered it up
with bright green paint
but one day walking
it started to rain
her heart turned blue
the green washed away
She covered it quickly
but She was too late
her blue heart was seen
thus was her fate
up walked a red heart
what could She do
She felt so ashamed
till She saw the blue
his heart was dripping
it too was wet
yes She saw a blue heart
under all the red
to walk in the rain
She would never regret
for that day She learned
two blues make a red

I CUT HER

I cut her

gingerly
demurely
without malice
never intent

I cut her

how could it be?
did She
stumble
trip
fall on me?

blood on my knife
a guileless blade

She bleeds
her lips in rage
her wounds
seep

it is my blame
a simple deed

a door
I closed

and with that

I cut her

SHE OF TOUCH

She of touch
holds me in place
the touch of eyes
caress my face
without a stroke
only in sound
a touch of voice
lays me down

She of touch
no longer here
I beg for hold
but no longer feel

She of touch
frozen in place
the touch of gone
now touching
my face

DEATH OF MY DREAMS

I now sit and mourn
the death of my dreams
although it was I
who did such a deed

I, just a nothing
quite undeserving
so I plunged the knife
a cruel act of hurting

dreams that tower
and always shine
do not belong
so they had to die

with blood on my hands
my head lowly hung
I morn for my dreams
and what I have done

I remember them well
they were once at hand
why they chose me
I could not comprehend

all that I wanted
all I could be
why did I kill them
and cause such grief

but what is disturbing
more than past sin
is if they returned
I would kill them
again

MY MUSE
IS CRUEL

my muse is cruel
She bends me at will
hand on my throat
She takes the wheel

into the corner
over the edge
wrecks me with sorrow
leaves me for dead

I pull myself out
I live through her sin
but before I can stand
She slams me again

strapped to carnage
filled with pain
her lust for destruction
knows no end

yes, my muse is cruel
so very unkind
to always stop short
of letting me die

SHE LEAVES
ME

I am yellow,
precaution -
She leaves me
disquieted

I am red,
titillation -
She leaves me
fervent

I am blue,
strangulation -
She leaves me
breathless

I am white,
asphyxiation -
She leaves me
dying

I am transparent,
insignificant -
without a word

She leaves
me

HEART A DAY

She broke
a heart a day.
all of them
mine.

KALYNN CAMPBELL

IN A TREE OF BLACK

with moss hangs
in a tree of black
the Shell of a life
a life taken back
thick branches hold
with ill intent
her gown of black silk
by a powder white neck
careless wind scatters
bright beams of moon
like a pyre of embers
quickly are strewn
blown to and fro
across the night
filling the air
glowing of firefly
they light her face
fixed are her eyes
the stare of a soul
too soon has died
hollow of secrets
gone to the grave
reflecting the sad
that couldn't be saved
dark hair flies
around her head kicks
strands wildly dance
over pale stillness
the cold ireful air
damp with death's chill
fawns at her face
licks at my tears
in a tree of black
I am the blame
from a necklace of rope
She hangs

HER EYES

you sit transfixed as
She pulls long strands of
shimmering honey-glazed
hair
from deep mysterious
eyes.
her eyes.
deep as stained mahogany
mesmerizing as the
northern lights.
her eyes.
they return your stare
with the radiance
of a thousand lit
stadium fields.
her eyes.
they look into your soul
like an x-ray
penetrating deep into a
buried tomb.
her eyes.
they read you with such
exacting precision.

you begin shrinking.

tiny.
inadequate.
unworthy.

her eyes.

if not for her
eyes.

MY MANY HEARTS

I have a heart to the north
and one to the west
one heart beats crimson
the other bright red
I had a heart of white
down by the sea
but a deceptive black tide
took it from me
I once had a pink heart
it came from the east
in a game of charades
I proved too weak
over a cyan ocean
beats a heart of green
it has no lock
so it can never be
down to the south
is a sad yellow heart
it wrapped me in tears
before having to part
an orange heart arrived
on a tepid blue day
orange hearts run wild
so they never stay

my own heart purple
once shot in a war
it takes all these colors
to beat red once more

SHE IS A WILLOW

She is a willow
a very sad tree
She is a willow
and quietly
She weeps
for me

She weeps in the night
She weeps in the day
She weeps in the snow
She weeps in the rain
She weeps out of sorrow
She weeps out of pain
She weeps till her weeping

brings me back

yet again

MY BROKEN WAYS

I am of the broken
in shadows I stay
this is my realm
my broken way

what do you seek
love or pain?
to those of the broken
both are the same

broken are flowers
stems bent in place
they grow in the garden
of broken ways

this poem is broken
rhymes walk lame
such is the child
of my broken ways

in this world I live
no perfection remains
for everything's created
of broken ways

WHY

why must I
remember
a love

She
forgot

I FELL

I fell
out of step
from day
into night
without struggle
or fight
I fell

out of life
out of the crowd
into the rain
I fell

mistaken was I
to myself
so into darkness
I fell

who was I
to fly

without wings
without sky
a leap
at a time
I fell

a push
or a shove
with help
above
I fell

where I lay
where I die
when I land
tell them

I fell

OUR END IS NEAR

no rain, not even a tear
for it is now written
our end is near

red in the sky
black in your eyes
loss will blow in
with a punishing goodbye

regret will soon cover
an angry sun
and strangle the two
that once were a one

I see it coming
on the horizon it looms
it foretells a death
it foretells our doom

but like you
I no longer care
it is what it is

our end is near

A SINGLE WORD

with a singe word
I deteriorate

woebegone
am I

love
heart
soul
She broke

with a single word

She desecrates

with a word
obliterates

now gone am I
Woebegone I stay

with a single word

She broke
away

WAITING

She clawed at my chest
ripped at my gate
tore at my fence
crumbled my wall
then took my hand

as if I had been
waiting
for her

KALYNN CAMPBELL

HER SILENCE

once it was golden
now cheap as steel
honed razor sharp
it stabs at my ears

cuts at my wrists
severs my heart...

it is her silence
and it chops me apart

things left unspoken
things never said
bitter words of silence
leave me for dead

they scream out at night
whisper through day
call out in silence
with nothing to say

they yell when it's quiet
they mummer in crowds

all without speaking
no, none of it out loud

it is her weapon
She uses it well

with a voice of silence
comes a deafening yell

AN ENDING

his loss brought you
his gain takes you away
your river of parting
was my ocean to pay

we strolled in a dream
but walked on a ledge
your love for us both
always on edge

i'll walk to safety
you continue this path
hold on to the belief
nothing good will last

and go kill our past
make me out as unkind
while I rhyme us an ending

goodbye in each line

HER NIGHT OUT

She looks stunning

in her broken halo
and torn self-esteem

She is made-up
for a date with herself
one She again

will break

AFTER HEAVEN FALLS

Into a wall of glass I walked
to cover weaknesses with scars
a fork I gave my soul mate
to eat my worthless heart

how in hell did I end up
eyes of an imperfect storm
to see my world collapsing
as worlds around me turn
regrets now choke the air
like dandelions of fall

this is life in shadows
after heaven falls

of me there is a secret
to the living I won't tell
it festers like a corpse
at the bottom of a well
and I've not spoken words
in all of twenty days
there is no purpose
i've nothing left to say
of pain I am reminded
I can't forget at all

this is life in shadows
after heaven falls

ANGEL OF
DROPPED WINGS

She of
avian kiss

angel of
dropped wings

I give of my
weakness
to feather
her needs

her heart
forgotten
clipped of flight

She of
avian kiss
and desire to fly

to me
tumbles
warm with touch
but chilled of ring

into my arms
angels fall
when they
drop
their wings

HER DIVE

I watched her
dive

it was not
as a swan

She did not
take flight

She simply
fell

into
the night

a dive
without grace

She simply
fell

away

from
me

KALYNN CAMPBELL

ANOTHER GOODBYE

behind -
the past bleeds
ahead -
the future weeps

with your goodbye
I take my leave

in love
I found pain
in pain my muse
but in goodbye
I found
you

there is no love
in deception
and no truth
in redemption

there was only proof
of your benighted crime
when I became
another
goodbye

behind -
yesterday bleeds
ahead -
tomorrow weeps
while today
reaps

another
goodbye

THE HIDDEN ONE

I am the hidden one
the shadow out of sight
it is I who quietly creeps
through black of night
I am the shape at the window
the movement on the wall
I am the call in the distance
the sound down the hall
the wind in your garden
the howl at midnight
I am the one that whispers
until you turn on the light
I remain with you
long after I'm gone
I am him
the hidden one

MEANINGLESS

She's seen
all She wants to see.
She knows
all She wants to know.
all else is meaningless.
She will never see
She will never know
how meaningless
She is
to all.

KALYNN CAMPBELL

SHE IS A CHEVRON

it is sewn onto her soul
stitched into her indolence
She is a chevron
a dictator
a demand
a war spilling from
armored eyes
and mortared lips
loathsomely Shelling
contemptuously embracing

She is vexation
with shrapnel arms
and grenade hands
barbed-wired hugs
feel for weakness
mining deep into flesh
explosive
volatile
this chevron
setting charges
trip wires
fulminating
her trigger nails
slice
abhorrently scar
carving words of
repugnance
into soft muscle of wound
subacid punctures

a cupid of dispraise
antagonistic war fairy
sutured with pretense
sown in antipathies

She is a chevron
and She demands a
capitulated
salute

THESE WORDS

these words I write
like stains on time
are from within
and spill with rhyme
but of my thoughts
the words are not
they are of a pain
within the heart
they come from She
a sadistic knife
She carves them deep
She gives them life
they are a burden
at times my noose
but I am helpless
what can I do
I have no choice
I can not fight
so of my She
these words
I write

KARMA

to you a toast
oh thee of
many thorn

at deception
you were masterful

and I
so slow
to learn

as I pick up
broken pieces
of your pillage
and plunder

I vow to make it
to the surface

in time to see you
go

under

HER RIVER

I saw her river rising
it came without warning
it came without rain
it came without thunder
it came without pain
it simply washed
our world
away

MY GARDEN OF SHE'S

long are the shadows
short are the days
quiet is the garden
in which I play

She of Self
I do not condemn
is swimming in lakes
of vanity again
She of Sun
once full of light
now lives in dark
embracing night
She of Art
who loved a thrill
spends her time
loving the guilt
She of Cat
with her gentle creep
now locked up tight
where he can see

all my She's
are scattered about
yet somehow call
without a sound
long is winter
short is life
sweet are these flowers
I will always prize

She of Thorn
i'll miss you least
it's hard to care
having been deceived

but soon is spring
when grows new seed
and flowers bloom
in my garden of She's

HER DEMONS

She took her love
but left her demons behind

oblique gifts of goodbye
abject parting forget-me-nots
farewell nothings
adieu to a bittersweet
love affair

the first is a blanket
woven of guilt
I am truly sorry I have it

the second is a narcissist
held captive in mirror
no matter how I try
I can't take my eyes off it

the third is indifference
just a tiny rock
it lodges in my bed and
my shoes with spiritless apathy
but I really don't care

although pitifully wretched
her demons are
they carry her sweet
angelic scent

they constantly remind me
of a time She was here
so it is I keep them
as my own

OF AGE

I never age yet I grow old
one day I will die young
having outlived myself

KALYNN CAMPBELL

HER BETRAYAL

quiet as I am
as quiet I be
the ease of your
betrayal
unsettles me

you played up a lie
it was a simple feat
how else could I
be kept at your feet

so go
be gone
with not a single care
where you are headed
a karma
awaits you there

yes, a hard rain
you will soon endure
perhaps that will soften
your rotten hard core

until then my love
remember this -
deception is as far
as the very next kiss

tell her She is wrong
this is her love song

I AM ENSLAVED

I am chattel
a detainee
I am the owned
her internee
I am the vassal
under black stiletto
the wild animal
She won't let go

I am enslaved
mind to body
an occupation
a soul seized

of the oppressed
an inmate of naught
for it is not me
my captor wants

MY WORLD
DIED

the day
my world died

I did not fight
I did not run
or take flight

I simply fell
came crashing down
until my heart
made not a sound

the day
my world died

SHE USED IT

I gave her an edge
She used it
    to cut me

I gave her the sun
She used it
    to blind me

I gave her my love
She
    used it

I AM A RIVER

I am a river
a ghost
adrift
while above
a bridge

takes
some one
home

once was a time
I thought
I could
spill

into the sea

past the
silt
to shores of
prosperity

but I got lost
on the banks
of this
adversity

among muck
and weeds
stranded
incomplete

forever adrift

in the river
of me

BLACK CLOUDS HANG

woe on the horizon
not far away
in a crestfallen sky
black clouds hang

the blue fell mirthless
behind doleful gray
with despair and gloom
black clouds hang

the wind blows mournful
air sullen and dank
forebodingly beckons
as Black clouds hang

how deep be their sorrow
how long dare they stay
nothing is certain
when Black clouds hang

HER WORDS

only once
can I
die

yet into
a grave
She drops me

with every
funereal
line

HITTING DESTINY

I can not stop
i'm moving too fast
you're in my lights
i've nowhere to pass
it's a hard kiss
we spin in the dark
intertwined by fate
connecting by spark
as our eyes meet
glass shatters with grace
both worlds collide
in a sudden embrace
this is no wreckage
no carnage here
no place of mourning
or shrine of tears
only a destiny
the way it was to be
I was racing to find you
as you were slowing
for me

KALYNN CAMPBELL

MY DEAD MUSE

I once had a muse
She loved and inspired
and in my art
lit a creative fire

on my shoulder
the amazing gift sat
until one gloomy day
She fell dead with a splat

it was so sad
my muse had died...
I grabbed a shovel
and headed outside

I dug and I dug
I dug up a mound
but a dead muse
wont stay in the ground

for every hole
I threw her in
that rotting dead muse
returned with a grin

the garbage I placed her
thought I'd see her no more
but a neighbors cat
dragged her to the door

then I saw kids
on their way to school
yes, I'll give her to them
they'd think She was cool

so I made a sign
'my muse for free'
but the kids only laughed
and kicked her at me

now I was angry
I had more than my fill
it was bad karma
but I'd give her to Goodwill

so off She went
like an old pair of socks
into the city
to a donation box

my life was again happy
although my art wasn't great
but I'd rather make crap
then own a muse I hate

two months later
a birthday came and went
with a cake and candles
and a gift a friend sent

the gift was stuffed
in a simple black bag
yes, it was my muse
with a goodwill price tag

so heed my warning
if your muse has died
don't try to dump her
don't think you can hide

one thing is clear
forever you're tied
you'll just have to hope
you are the first
to die

MY POISON

She is my poison.
my destruction.
you know this.
yet She is everywhere.
you see me shoot her under my skin.
you hear me fill my lungs with her when we are in bed.
still, you feign the poison is not in our house.
but we both know better.
you know better.
the poison finds its way into my hands with ease
for you are the one who spreads the poison.
how could I miss it?
you are wearing her perfume.
you style your hair as hers.
you call me the pet name she did.
you are the one controlling the poison.
and I am slowly dying.
why do you place her in my hands?
to poison my heart?
no.
it is not about me.
you don't care if She kills me.
you want her to kill us.
strangle us.
dead.
so you feed her to me.
a dose at a time.
yes, She is my poison.
but you are our
destruction.

KALYNN CAMPBELL

THE FLOOD (PARTS I & II)

I.

I awoke to her weeping
She wept for her dreams
a weeping of forever
and forever it seemed
and with every tear
down came the rain
till the river moaned
swollen with pain
the harder it rained
the more She wept
the river then breached
flood waters dense
swirling around
her tears like a spell
sweeping me under
into a coma I fell...

She wept me a river
She wept me a flood
entombed us in water
drowning our love

II.

I awoke to stillness
no weeping or rain
no dark of sky
or flowing of pain
the river ran quiet
the flood was gone
and She with it
I was now all alone
I wandered the streets
called out her name
but everything's gone
no, nothing remains
somewhere She sits
and weeps of dreams
dreams of forever
and forever it seems
and wherever She is
I wish her well
to bring such rain
She knows much hell
a grave, our past
the flood, our time
so softly I mourn
and leave it behind
washed in her sorrow
baptized in pain
I am haunted by nothing
for nothing remains

HER SUNSET

She of thorn
in sun of red
clings to night
her blue long dead

over gloaming sky
stops and hangs
in sundown rage
screams my name

rancorous horizon
welkin of thorn
She of red
sun of blood
hangs

the sky ablaze
I beg of She

to just
set

THEY ARE TREES

trees
my family
and friends were

like the spruce
and pines
of a christmas

as days fell
behind

green turned
away
branches
grew stark

needles
dropped

into memory

until
came the day

all that
remained

a
single
solitary
wreath

of goodbyes

IN WORDS

of She I write
in me She speaks
even with that
She shows
disdain
for me

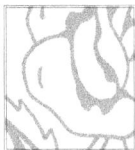

SHE IS A TRAP

She is a trap
the truth in her hold
desperate
clinging
poaching shallow
setting cages
inhumanly devised
baited of contemptible
desire
and repugnant
lies

She of trap
the killing kind
cunningly
ruthless
knifes for eyes

cutting deep
this her libation
her lips slowly part
as She begins
the evisceration
straight
to the heart
cracked with precision
bled with rigor
skilled at the sever
cruel in the slay
She is a trap
laying in wait

and I
her kill

THE GIRL WHO DIED

I.

there once was a girl
who came to stay
why with me
I can not say

She did not call
She did not knock
She simply moved in
and changed the locks

her art went up
on every wall
in every corner
She placed a doll

wherever I went
She followed me there
She became my shadow
it was quite queer

She stuck hearts
on all my clothes
She covered the mirrors
with Swedish prose

then one day
She started to speak
I was surprised
for She was quite meek

II.

She whispered low
I strained to hear
what She said
struck me with fear

She said She brought
eighty-nine goodbyes
and it was with me
She had come to die

so once a day
She would say goodbye
and once a day
She pretended to die

on and on
this would repeat
She would say goodbye
then lay at my feet

the days soon past
quickly went by
until it was time
for the ninetieth goodbye

IV.

I was stunned
as She walked out the door
She didn't die
what was it for?

on the mirror
a short piece of prose
it was in Swedish
so I had to transpose

'yes, my death
was a day at a time
because I knew
you would never be mine'

short and simple
that's all it said
I closed my eyes
and lowered my head

I felt so alone
I began to cry
because I now wanted
the girl who died.

III.

I was worried
my world was blue
I wish She'd die elsewhere
it was cold but true

from the hallway
that girl who appeared
walked to me slow
her eyes wet from tears

yes, I knew
She would whisper goodbye
but unlike before
She would actually die

She touch my hand
and kissed my face
"goodbye" She said
with a last embrace

quickly She turned
then gathered her art
picked up the dolls
and took all the hearts

THE REASONS

soon I must reap
my words
sown dreams
have faded into
the grave
with a blunt knife
I spread myself thin
over yet another
hollow today

a figure of once
I am but residue
a still-life
not of repose
for of me
I subsume

my invisible life
never expires
although an anima
weak of morale
constantly
tires

so on the edge
forever I walk
having let her heart
nail my soul
to another
soulless cross

yes, spit my name
and make a wish
for desperate are lips
of the never kissed
and too fast I lived
while moving too slow

these are the reasons
I must reap
the words
I sow

KALYNN CAMPBELL

THE GOSPEL OF GOODBYE

melancholy broke
late in the night
fever withered
died

a monumental event
downplayed
without melopoeia
She quietly fades

scars of euphonic braille
mellifluous musical notes
fingers strum
stroke
corporeal Sheet music
of tattooed skin

I, a cacophonous gospel
a hymn...

goodbye
halo of tears
poetic muse
goodbye
my She
my sadness
my grief
my love
my hate
my worship
my pain

the wound
now of the grave
I pray

goodbye She

forever
you'll haunt me

goodbye.

ETERNALLY
YOURS

She showed me
there was beauty
in the beginning
of every
end.

SHE OF THORN represents the collected poetry and prose of Kalynn Campbell. Many of the poems originally appeared on his Instagram account from January 2014 to February 2015. All ties between Campbell and the 'She' referred to in the introduction were severed in early January after three years of "tumultuous" communication. 'She' supported the publication of SHE OF THORN but requested her name be withheld. The author and publisher both respect her request.

Kalynn Campbell, a Los Angeles painter, illustrator, and writer is one of the early artists in the 'lowbrow/pop surrealism' art movement. He began showing his work in the early 1990's at the seminal ZERO ONE GALLERY on Melrose Avenue in Los Angeles.

Campbell's paintings and prints have been featured in six Museum shows (including the pivotal Multi City KUSTOM KULTURE show, The Colorado POP SURREALISM show and the Los Angeles 100 ARTISTS SEE SATAN show) and numerous art galleries.

Books and Magazines featuring his work are numerous, among them, POP SURREALISM by Kristin Anderson, WEIRDO DELUXE by Matt Dukes Jordan and KUSTOM GRAPHICS 2 from Korero.
Collectors include Actor Nicholas Cage, Rocker Eric Burden, Singer Pink and Simpson's voice man Harry Shearer.
His illustration work has been utilized by a virtual who's who of rock music, from punk startup Epitaph Records to Megadeth and Tom Petty.
Campbell's work has graced a long line of signature products; lighters, belt buckles, skateboard wheels, guitar straps and even blue-tooth phone sets. Currently he has a line of stickers and decals available from YUJEAN.

For almost ten years Campbell was key cartoonist for counterculture guru Paul Krassner, illustrating political cartoons for Krassner's REALIST magazine. Campbell's work from the magazine is among those featured in a Fantagraphics book due for publication Fall 2015.

Campbell has written two novels, IN THE TIME OF THE FLY and THE MUSE, both scheduled for release in 2015. He has AvPD and lives a reclusive lifestyle in Los Angeles.

campbell@SheOfThorn.com

Visit: **www.SheOfThorn.com** for She books & poem wear

The entirety of this book designed and illustrated
by Kalynn Campbell and Roulette Studios
www.roulettestudios.com
in conjunction with
Torn Apart Books, Los Angeles - www.tornapartbooks.com
All content copyright © 2015 Kalynn Campbell

THORN of LOVE

www.ingramcontent.com/pod-product-compliance
Lightning Source LLC
Chambersburg PA
CBHW060018050426
42448CB00012B/2806